Jules Verne and the First Science Fiction Masquerade

Jules Verne
and the First Science Fiction Masquerade

Kathe Gust

How the Father of Science Fiction Literature organized the first science fiction-themed masquerade sixty years before the advent of the costumed science fiction convention.

Produced in the United States of America.
Location of Publication: Redwood City, California, USA.
Publication Date: March 2026.
Publisher: International Costumers' Guild Press.
Cover Design: Philip Gust.

ISBN 978-1-966384-09-0 (Softcover)
ISBN 978-1-966384-10-6 (Hardcover)
ISBN 978-1-966384-11-3 (eBook)
ISBN 978-1-966384-12-0 (Audiobook)

Library of Congress Control Number: 2026937254

"If I'm too hot, I go up. If I'm too cold, I come down. If I meet an impassable mountain, I fly above it; a precipice, I sail over it; a river, I float across it."

Dr. Samuel Fergusson, *Five Weeks in a Balloon*

CONTENTS

A little over a year ago, the author, Kathe Gust, saw a reproduction of an illustration from the French newspaper *Le Monde Illustré* about a masquerade ball put on in 1877 by science fiction pioneer Jules Verne. She knew that costumed masquerades were popular in the 19th century, but what caught her attention was that attendees seemed to be wearing costumes inspired by Jules Verne's novels.

The common wisdom is that the first costumed science fiction-themed convention did not take place until over sixty years later, at the first Worldcon in 1939. Had Jules Verne once again anticipated the future?

As a professional research librarian, as well as an avid science fiction and historical costumer and cosplayer, Kathe decided to learn more about the event. She found that there was almost nothing written in English about why it was held and what kinds of costumes were worn, and only scattered references in letters and newspapers of the time that were all in French.

Digging deeper, she uncovered a remarkable story about how Jules Verne's popularity as the first author of the genre then known as "scientific fiction," and his connection to his adopted home town of Amiens, France where he had met his wife, lead him to organize a costumed masquerade ball as a way of introducing his family to the society of the city. She also discovered a second costumed masquerade he put on several years later that was inspired by his novels.

Based on her in-depth research, Kathe wove together the material she gathered into the story of what are arguably the first science fiction-themed costumed masquerades ever held, where hundreds of attendees dressed in Verne's honor, inspired by characters and places in his novels. He was also, in modern parlance, the first "Author Guest of Honor," a role that is now common at science fiction conventions.

In addition to telling this remarkable story, Kathe also presents historical photos and illustrations from the time, including full-color plates that are not widely available. She includes her translations of some of the texts that she used, as well as citations and bibliographic references, and a full index to help readers locate topics and people in the text.

This book is not only an interesting story from a human perspective, but also sheds light on the history of early science fiction literature, and costumed masquerade balls that were popular in the 19th century. It provides new insight into the man who is widely regarded as the Father of Science Fiction Literature.

Philip Gust,

Author of *Myrtle R Douglas: Mother of Convention Costuming* (ICG Press, 2025).

February 2026

JULES VERNE AND THE DAWN OF SCI-FI LITERATURE

During the 1860's, France was one of the hubs of advancements in science as well as literature. Pasteur was working on pasteurization and vaccination. Berthelot was working on synthetic and thermochemistry. Science was moving out of Paris as other cities developed into centers for metallurgy, chemistry, photography and medicine. There was strong public interest in scientific progress, which was beginning to be reflected in literature and art. Significant authors were experimenting with social dramas, symbolism, and realism.

It was in this environment that Jules Verne became the pioneer of what was then called "scientific fiction." Verne was born in 1828 and studied to become a lawyer like his father. His first big success as a professional author was *Cinq Semaines en Ballon* (*Five Weeks in a Balloon*), which became a best-seller when it was published in 1863. It was a new kind of story, one that combined scientific fact with adventure fiction.

Verne was not a scientist, and had no experience with balloons when he wrote the story. "I wrote *Five Weeks in a Balloon* not as a story about ballooning, but as a story about Africa," he said in an 1884 interview. [9] "I always was greatly interested in geography and travel, and I wanted to give a romantic description of Africa. Now, there was no means of taking my travelers through Africa otherwise than in a balloon, and that is why a balloon is introduced."

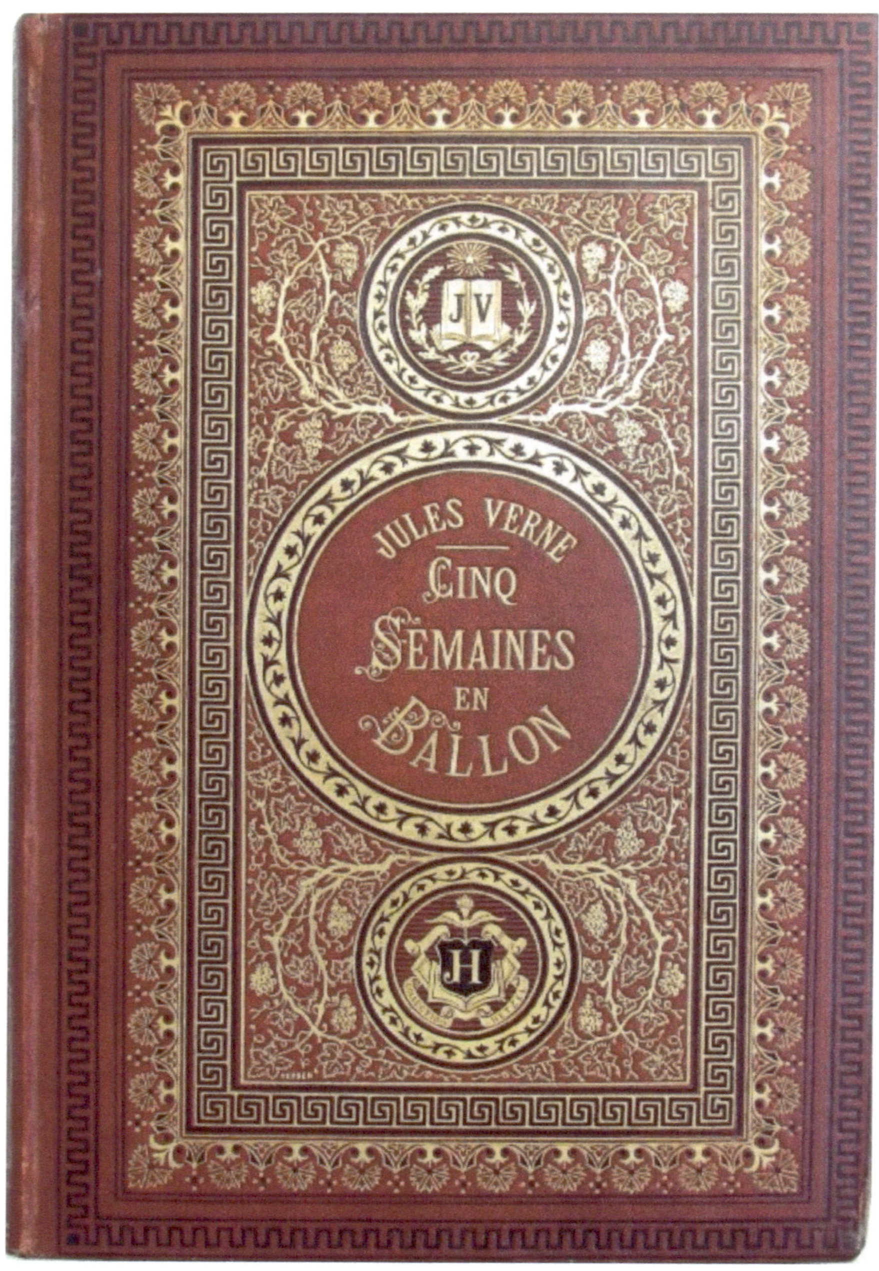

Early French edition of Verne's first book, Five Weeks in a Balloon, *published by Pierre-Jules Hetzel, c. 1880.*

4   Jules Verne and the First Science Fiction Masquerade

In September 1862 Verne had met Pierre-Jules Hetzel, who agreed to publish the book. It was also serialized in the French magazine *Le Magasin d'éducation et de recreation* (*The Magazine of Education and Recreation*). Founded by Hetzel and Jean Macé, the magazine featured many of Verne's works, either before or at the same time they were released as books, a common practice in the 19th century.

Hetzel offered Verne a long-term, exclusive contract with a steady salary in exchange for at first two, and then three, works of "scientific fiction" per year for 20 years. Verne became a full-time writer, and so began a highly successful author-publisher collaboration that lasted for more than 40 years.

The collaboration resulted in over 60 works, 54 of them making up the popular *Voyages Extraordinaires* (*Extraordinary Voyages*) series of "geographical novels" that Verne wrote to map out the world's knowledge. The series includes some of Verne's best-known titles, such as *Journey to the Center of the Earth, From the Earth to the Moon, Twenty Thousand Leagues Under the Seas,* and *The Mysterious Island.*

Verne's contract with Hetzel meant that he did not directly share in the profits from the tremendous popularity of his books. They were essentially works for hire, though he later renegotiated for a higher salary. However, his contract gave Verne rights to other uses of his stories and characters, so he decided to adapt them for the stage.

Starting in 1849, prior to his novels, Verne had been a prolific playwright in Paris, writing plays, comedies, and light opera librettos. Fueled by the

Théâtre du Châtelet. Around the World in 80 Days, *Emile Leavy & Cie (Paris) 1886.*

public's enthusiasm for his books, his stage adaptations were equally popular. Verne's wealth primarily came not from his books, but from the revenue and royalties from his plays. As he said in an 1894 interview, "I adored the stage and all connected with it, and writing plays is still the work that gives me the most pleasure." [9]

Normally Verne had a quiet, methodical work habit. He generally rose at 5 a.m. and wrote until eleven. Then he would read "from cover to cover" fifteen different newspapers, taking notes, sometimes attended professional meetings, and was in bed by 9 p.m.

New works by Verne continued to be published well after his death in 1905. He had left a drawerful of nearly completed manuscripts that were "edited" by his son, Michel. Verne has become the second most translated author in the world, after Agatha Christie and ahead of William Shakespeare, although many of the early English translations are felt by critics, and Verne himself, not to capture his actual style. [9]

Jules Verne by his friend, Gaspard-Félix Tournachon, known as Nadar, c. 1878, Oil paint over photograph.

JULES VERNE THROWS A SCI-FI THEMED MASQUERADE BALL

Extravagant costumed masquerade balls in the 19th century were the high point of society entertainments, attended by an amazing array of fanciful costumed characters. This was an international social fashion in Britain, Europe, and North America. During this time, the opportunity to reimagine oneself as an alter ego was treated as the chance of a lifetime, and required both some study and some expense for members of high society.

Masquerade balls served as way for the upper classes to showcase their wealth, express themselves, and engage in a form of playful fantasy, yet remain within the strict social rules of the time. Their costumes were often elaborate and expensively created by couturiers like the House of Worth.

These events were also widely reported in society pages as news, making them a public display of status, and a way for hostesses to gain social prestige. For one evening, guests transformed themselves into characters usually inspired by history, fantasy, or the works of famous artists, depending on the theme of the event.

In 1857, Verne married Honorine Anne Hébée Morel (née du Fraysne de Viane), who he had met on a visit to Amiens in 1856. She was a 26 year old widow with two daughters; their son, Michel was born in 1861. The family resided in Paris until they moved to Honorine's home town in 1871 to be closer to her family, and bought a house.

Turkish style costume, c. 1870. House of Worth. Photo: Metropolitan Museum of Art.

According to Verne, "Family ties and the quiet of the place have bound me to Amiens ever since." [9] It was while living there that Verne wrote the majority of his works.

Several years later, in April 1877, the Vernes hosted the first of two costumed masquerade balls that may have been the first to be inspired by what we now call science fiction or sci-fi literature. It was an elaborate event that was themed around his novel *From the Earth to the Moon*.

They sent out 700 invitations for the event. "Mr. and Mrs. Jules Verne [to quote the invitation] thank in advance those of their guests who would like to come in costume for this dance." [1]. Many of the more than 350 guests who attended did dress as characters or from locations in his popular *Voyages Extraordinaires* (*Extraordinary Voyages*) series.

The Verne family lived a relatively modest upper middle-class life, but Verne, though somewhat shy, actually enjoyed hosting social gatherings. Many town residents attended the various soirées and receptions he hosted at his second residence at 2, rue Charles-Dubois, sometimes called the House with the Tower. It is now the Maison de Jules Verne Museum.

This ball would be something more, much more. Verne claimed that he spent 4,000 francs on the evening. Based on historical exchange rates, gold value, and inflation, one French franc from 1877 is worth roughly $3.50 to $4.00 USD in 2025 purchasing power. That sum included the rental of a hall large enough to hold fifteen hundred people, and decorations worthy of a carnival. [1]

Jules Verne house at 2, rue Charles-Dubois, c. 1894.

According to the newspaper *Le Monde Illustré* (*The Illustrated World*), Verne's Grand Masquerade Ball took place at the Salons Saint-Denis, and was a significant social event, as the local town was abuzz with anticipation. It was fully covered by the *Le Monde Illustré* with an engraving of some of the evening's delights.

They reported, "Monsieur Jules Verne has already discovered how to control balloons, travel twenty thousand leagues under the sea, penetrate the center of the Earth, and travel around the Moon. He has just attempted a perhaps even more difficult undertaking. He has imagined putting into action—in Amiens!—a tale from the Arabian Nights. In other words, he invited the inhabitants of the city where he has taken up residence to take part in a costume ball".

Verne's compatriots did not hesitate to respond to the famous novelist's invitation. Based on further reporting, the guest list continued to grow. The Amiens newspapers tell us that the party, given on Easter Monday, April 2, 1877, exceeded all possible splendor.

"The Saint-Denis salons, magnificently decorated, were prepared to accommodate more than fifteen hundred people. The ball began at ten o'clock, and at that moment, the view was magical. The costumes, remarkably rich, were interspersed with those taken from the works of the master of the house, to whom it was important to pay a shining tribute by reproducing the different types created by his fertile imagination.

Engraving from Le Monde Illustré *illustrating some of the evening's delights.*

Engraving from Le Monde Illustré *illustrating some of the evening's delights.*

"Among the ladies, there were Indian costumes of great value and perfectly executed; fashionable pieces provided many subjects, including a ravishing Marjolaine. The men wore Mexican, Chinese, Arab, Russian, and other costumes; noteworthy is a Pierrot costume, which, although very simple and in good taste, cost only 1,800 francs [$6,300-$7,200 USD today]. Needless to say, the Offenbach carabinieri detachment performed marvelously, and were perfectly cast; the rural policeman who commanded them was without equal; a true creation.

"The ball ended with a very varied cotillion that didn't end until six o'clock in the morning. This celebration will tour the world via *Le Monde Illustré*."

At least 200 of the guests were reported to have come in costume, including Verne's close friend Gaspard-Félix Tournachon, known as Nadar, who was the model for Michel Ardan, the hero of his novels *From the Earth to the Moon* and *Around the Moon*, He came disguised as that character. [2]

Among the highlights of the evening, Nadar emerged from a munitions shell that had been rolled into the middle of the quadrille. [3] Such a shell was used in *From the Earth to the Moon* to launch the explorers from a giant cannon on their voyage

Nadar, a French photographer, caricaturist, journalist, novelist, and balloonist, was also a proponent of heavier-than-air flight. In 1858, he became the first person to take aerial photographs from a balloon.

Illustration of munitions shell from From the Earth to the Moon *by Jules Verne drawn by Henri de Montaut, 1868. This was the inspiration for Verne's friend Nadar's skit at Verne's 1877 masquerade ball.*

Nadar elevating photography to a high art. Lithograph by Honoré Daumier, 1862. Nadar combined his love of photography and ballooning to pioneer the field of aerial photography.

18   Jules Verne and the First Science Fiction Masquerade

It was also reported, "In the assembly, one recognizes Captain Nemo, Professor Lidenbrock, Phileas Fogg, Passepartout, Michael Strogoff: all of Verne's characters... On vast tapestries are painted the 'Nautilus,' the 'Albatross,' the 'Victoria.' To the sound of the orchestra, Native Americans, aeronauts, Maharanis, bears, and monkeys run wild."

In a letter to his publisher and friend Pierre-Jules Hetzel dated March 11, 1877, Verne described the upcoming evening as follows:

"Imaginez-vous que le lundi de Pâques, nous donnons un bal travesti à Amiens. 700 invitations lancées, 350 acceptations au moins. Toute la ville en rumeur." ("Imagine that on Easter Monday, we are giving a costume ball in Amiens. 700 invitations sent out, at least 350 accepted. The whole town is in a frenzy.") [4]

The ball's main purpose had been to offer a chance to introduce his 15 year-old son, Michel to local high society, but it was also an opportunity for Honorine to revive her personal prestige. It seems that the Verne family felt Amiens society, which had viewed Madame Verne as an ornament when she was younger, was somewhat ignoring her now that she had returned

Sadly, Honorine, who may even have come up with the idea for the ball, was severely ill and unable to attend. A few days after it took place, Verne expressed his disappointment in another letter to Hetzel:

"When you live among provincials, you have to do as the provincials do. Hence, the ball in question, which was magnificent. By giving it, I knew I was giving my wife the greatest pleasure... and my wife couldn't attend! You can imagine the heartbreak! I was the only one who could have given this ball in Amiens in this form. For 35 years, there hadn't been a costume ball in the city. My name, which is neutral, brought together a very distinguished company that no political or industrial name could have rallied...

"You know perfectly well, partially, why I'm in Amiens. Life in Paris with my wife, as you are aware, was impossible. Well, I did as the Romans do, but there are no regrets... it would have been perfect... if my wife could have come. As for postponing the party, that was impossible, because people were coming from neighboring towns and from Paris." [5]

For Verne, the sensation created by this costumed masquerade ball was beyond his expectation, as hundreds of attendees honored him by appearing richly-costumed as characters or from locations in his books. It was only marred by the fact that his dear wife was not able to attend and share in the excitement and triumph. One can only imagine Honorine's disappointment at missing this grand event. He would have to think of something to make it up to her.

The heartbreak of Verne's wife, Honorine being unable to attend the first ball might have been what led to another similar event held seven years later at the home he purchased in 1882 at 2, rue Charles-Dubois. It was held on March 8, 1885 in celebration of the Verne's 28th wedding anniversary. [6] It was recorded at the time that the Vernes frequently entertained, but it was not normally on such a lavish scale as that first costumed masquerade ball.

This second ball that he and his wife gave had the theme of "La Grande Auberge du Tour du Monde" or "The Great Inn of the Trip Around the World." The inspiration for the theme seems to have been his extremely popular book, *Around the World in 80 Days*, which had been published in serial form in 1872, ten years earlier.

This time Honorine was in good health and able to be present. For this event, Verne and his wife were costumed as the Innkeepers. Jules was the host, dressed as a butcher, and both received the approximately 200 guests in their grand salon, which had been re-decorated as a tavern. Honorine was observed stirring the pot-au-feu in a huge kettle, but in actuality, a caterer had been engaged. [6]

The guests were expected to wear traditional costumes from the many countries that were visited by the novel's protagonist Phileas Fogg and his companion Passepartout. Verne later recalled the impetus for the book. "One day in a Paris café, I read in *Le Siècle* [*The*

Century] that a man could travel round the world in eighty days. It immediately struck me that I could profit by a difference of meridian and make my traveler gain or lose a day in his journey. There was my dénouement ready found." [9]

Drawing by 19th century French cartoonist Gédéon Baril for Verne's 1885 masquerade ball.

No invitations to this party have survived, but a poster nearly two meters (six and a half feet) high, designed by Verne's friend, 19th century French cartoonist Gédéon Baril, was displayed at the entrance to the salon on rue Charles-Dubois during the party. Translated into English, it says, "The Grrrreat Inn of the Trip Around the World, run by Mr. and Mrs. Jules Verne. For today only, drinks are free."

Exotic international-themed costumes were not uncommon for masquerade balls of the 19th century, but this ball was notable because many attendees intentionally wore costumes that were chosen based on locations mentioned in Verne's science fiction novel. Once again, their balloonist, caricaturist, photographer friend, Nadar was in attendance dressed as Michel Ardan, the character he inspired in Verne's earlier novels, *From the Earth to the Moon* and *Around the Moon*.

This second masquerade ball was a success, and solidified the Verne's social standing. Their place in Amiens society that they had longed for after they moved to the city was secure.

Verne himself was adopted by the city as their very own famous author, and was held in widespread respect and admiration. He was elected as a permanent member of the Académie des Sciences, Lettres et Arts d'Amiens (Amiens Academy of Sciences, Literature and Arts) in 1872 and served as its annual director in 1875 and 1881.

Verne was also elected city councilor in 1888 and served for 16 years, until 1904, overseeing a number of public works projects. His funeral in 1905 became a major municipal celebration of his genius and his place in their society.

Poster by 19th century French cartoonist Gédéon Baril for Verne's 1885 masquerade ball.

Jules Verne funeral procession in Amiens, 1905. Verne's Son Michel and grandson are in the front row. Photo: Étienne Carjat.

Despite his warm embrace by his adopted city, the form of scientific fiction and adventure literature that he created was looked on skeptically by the French literary community. The Académie Française (French Academy) in Paris dismissed his immensely popular *Voyages Extraordinaires* series of novels as mere "children's literature" or "scientific tales" rather than serious, artistic literature. They never accepted him as a member, despite repeated endorsements from French literary luminaries such as his friend, Victor Hugo. "The great regret of my life is that I have never taken any place in French literature." [9]

Jules and Honorine Verne, 1900. Photo: L'Illustration, *a French weekly magazine.*

JULES VERNE-INSPIRED ATTRACTIONS AND MERCHANDISE

In the 20th century, holding major costume events based on themes from Verne's stories were less frequent, but that does not mean he was no longer providing inspiration. Although no single major Jules Verne-themed party appears to have been held, his works did inspire gatherings, particularly via Steampunk culture that emerged in the late 20th century, science fiction conventions, a few themed events such as the Carnegie Museum's "Around the World" fund raiser, and personal parties and themed weddings.

The actual Maison de Jules Verne Museum in Amiens began offering a chance to visit the festive Grand Auberge experience back in 2006. Once a year, a work by the author was celebrated with a small evening party based on a particular country. China, Africa, Russia, and even Transylvania were produced. The staff wore traditional costumes, provided cultural experiences, and native foods for a truly immersive experience. Whether the COVID-19 pandemic from 2020 to 2023 put an end to this summer event, I was unable discover. [8]

Both a restaurant at the Eiffel Tower and hotel in France have Jules Verne as the main theme, and an entire "land" at Disneyland Paris is based on the writer's works, as well as a section of Disneyland Tokyo celebrating *Journey to the Center of the Earth*.

Disneyland Tokyo Journey to the Center of the Earth *attraction. Photo: Walt Disney Company.*

There is even a complete theme park. Jules Verne's *Around the World in Eighty Days* inspired the creation of the Worlds of Fun theme park in Kansas City, Missouri, featuring lands like Americana, Europa, Africa, Scandinavia and Orient reflecting the book's journey.

There is also Jules Verne themed merchandise. Lego produced a blocks set based on details of *Around the World in Eighty Days*, *Twenty Thousand Leagues Under the Seas*, and *Five Weeks in a Balloon*, three of Verne's most popular novels.

Lego set based on three of Verne's most popular works.

Even in Verne's time, toy makers looked to profit from the popularity of his stories, such as board games that used illustrations of characters and locations mentioned in his novels.

But not all is happiness and cheer. In 2016, a student committee from a Cambridge University college cancelled a party themed on *Around the World in 80 Days* because of worries that the event had the "potential for offence" due to "cultural appropriation" and could even be seen as racist if students dressed in clothes from different cultures, according to an article in the student newspaper, *The Cambridge Tab*. [10]

Game of Goose board game inspired by Around the World in 80 Days *(1880-90).*

The writer of the article went on to castigate the Pembroke College student committee for its action. "My basic argument is this; most of the rhetoric surrounding cultural appropriation is misguided and wrong. The idea that people's cultures can be appropriated is based on political ideals of segregation and self-interest, and it is immensely damaging for racial integration in general. What's more, it is an insult to me and many other mixed-race people like me."

So, what do you think? Do Jules Verne's masquerade balls represent the first costumed science fiction-themed events? They both were based on his "scientific fiction" novels, many of the guests wore costumes inspired by characters or locations in his books, and one even enacted a skit.

In my opinion, his first ball in 1877 certainly counts, and came sixty years before the 1939 World Science Fiction Convention (Nycon I), where two attendees wore the first costumes at a modern science fiction-themed convention. They were inspired by the 1936 movie *Things to Come*, based on a science fiction novel by H. G. Wells. [11]

Some might argue that the second ball in 1885 does not count because, although the theme was based on Verne's book, *Around the World in 80 Days*, the emphasis was on countries of the world rather than characters in the book.

However Verne himself said that his great interest was in geography and that he simply used scientific means in his books as a way to explore places. "My object has been to depict the earth, and not the earth alone, but the universe, for I have sometimes taken my readers away from earth, in the novel." [9]

Nycon I in 1939 had "The World of Tomorrow" as its theme. The two costumes worn there were inspired not by specific characters in Wells' book or the movie, but by the aesthetic of that futuristic world. Perhaps the second Verne ball counts too.

Where do you stand on the question?

Forest J Ackerman and Myrtle R Douglas wore costumes at Nycon I in 1939, inspired by the 1936 movie Things to Come. *Colorization by the International Costumers' Guild Archives of a 1939 photo by Charles Horning matches known colors of their costumes.*

There are no photographs, indeed very little information beyond the few mentions in letters and reports, about the Verne's masquerade balls. Fortunately, there are some contemporary sources where we can still garner some idea of the costumes that may have been worn.

Three books published during Verne's lifetime on what was then called "fancy dress" are available for browsing online.

Fancy Dresses Described: Or, What to Wear at Fancy Balls by Ardern Holt,

> 3rd greatly enlarged ed. 1882.
> *https://babel.hathitrust.org/cgi/pt?id=nyp.33433072177276&seq=9*

> 5th ed. 1887.
> *https://archive.org/details/fancydressesdesc00holt/mode/2up*

> 6th ed. 1896.
> *https://archive.org/details/gri_33125002201586/mode/2up*

Gentlemen's Fancy Dress: How to Choose It by Ardern Holt, 1882.
https://www.google.com/books/edition/Gentlemen_s_Fancy_Dress/ED8CAAAAQAAJ

Characters Suitable for Fancy Costume Balls by Marie Schild, 1881.
https://books.google.co.zm/books?id=oy8BAAAAQAAJ

These books describe a great many costume options and have sketches of some of them. Later editions of *Fancy Dresses Described* even have some full-page color plates.

Searching online has also turned up some photographs of comparable events where photographs were taken. These can give us additional ideas of the costumes of that time.

French costume ball, May 29, 1891. Photo by Paul Nadar.

Perhaps one of the best sources is the costume collection at the McCord Stewart Museum in Montreal, Canada. They have photographs and even some costumes from the era, worn by people who were attending various costume balls, and have held a past exhibition of them that ran from November 14, 2024, to August 17, 2025.

Although it was not the main intent to document costumes worn to those lavish costume balls and skating carnivals held in the late 19th century, there were many on display of the type that might have been worn to the Verne balls.

https://www.musee-mccord-stewart.ca/en/exhibitions/costume-balls/

J. S. Wilson's costumed group, Montreal, QC, 1870. Photo courtesy of McCord Stewart Museum.

On the following pages are examples from two editions of Ardern Holt's book, *Fancy Dresses Described: Or, What to Wear at Fancy Balls* that represent the kinds of fancy dress costumes that might have been worn at Jules Verne's balls.

Armenian Girl. Fancy Dresses Described: Or, What to Wear at Fancy Balls *by Arden Holt. (1896) Paris.*

Italian Girl. Fancy Dresses Described: Or, What to Wear at Fancy Balls *by Arden Holt. (1887) Paris*

Incroyable French Girl. Fancy Dresses Described: Or, What to Wear at Fancy Balls *by Arden Holt. (1887) Paris.*

Springtime in Japan. Fancy Dresses Described: Or, What to Wear at Fancy Balls *by Arden Holt. (1896) Paris*

Swiss Girl. Fancy Dresses Described: Or, What to Wear at Fancy Balls *by Arden Holt. (1887) Paris*

40 Jules Verne and the First Science Fiction Masquerade

Scotch Fishwife. Fancy Dresses Described: Or, What to Wear at Fancy Balls *by Arden Holt. (1896) Paris*

Monte Carlo Girl. Fancy Dresses Described: Or, What to Wear at Fancy Balls *by Arden Holt. (1887) Paris*

42 Jules Verne and the First Science Fiction Masquerade

Normandy France Girl. Fancy Dresses Described: Or, What to Wear at Fancy Balls *by Arden Holt. (1887) Paris*

Classical Greco-Roman. Fancy Dresses Described: Or, What to Wear at Fancy Balls *by Arden Holt. (1887) Paris*

44 Jules Verne and the First Science Fiction Masquerade

1. Herbert R Lottman, *Jules Verne*, Flammarion, 1996, Page 231

2. Jean-Paul Dekiss, *Jules Verne, The Enchanter*, Éditions du Félin, 1999, p. 227

3. Simone Vierne, *Jules Verne and the Initiatory Novel*, Éditions du Syrac, 1973, p. 473

4. Saint Bris, Gonzague, *Sur les pas de Jules Verne*, Presses de la renaissance, 2005. p. 78

5. Letter dated March 11, 1877 quoted from Olivier Dumas, Volker Dehs, and Piero Gondolo della Riva, *Correspondance inédite*, op. cit. p. 159.

6. Letter dated April 1877 quoted from Eric Weissenberg, *Jules Verne : un univers fabuleux*, Favre, 2004, p. 204.

7. Olivier Dumas, *Jules Verne,* La Manufacture, 1988, p. 148-49.

8. Alix Penichou, "A ball at Jules Verne's house, almost like in his time," *L'Action Agricole Picarde*, August 4, 2018.

9. R. H. Sherard, "Jules Verne at Home: His Own Account of his Life and Work," *McClure's Magazine*, January 1894.

https://www.excellence-in-literature.com/jules-verne-at-home-1894-interview-by-sherard/

10. Alex Stride, "Around the World bop: Perhaps we should toast Cultural Approp," *The Tab*, Cambridge, March 12, 2016.

    https://archive.thetab.com/uk/cambridge/2016/03/12/pembroke-bop-cult-approp-72722

11. Philip Gust, *Myrtle R Douglas: Mother of Convention Costuming*, International Costumers' Guild Press, 2025.

    https://costume.org/wp/2025/01/07/myrtle-r-douglas-mother-of-convention-costuming/

A

Académie des Sciences, Lettres et Arts d'Amiens · *See* Amiens Academy of Sciences, Literature and Arts
Albatross · 19
Amiens · 1, 9, 11, 13, 19, 20, 23, 25, 27
Amiens Academy of Sciences, Literature and Arts · 23
Around the Moon · 16, 23
Around the World in 80 Days · 6, 21, 29, 30, 31

B

Baril, Gédéon · 22, 23, 24

C

Cambridge University · 29
Captain Nemo · 19
Cinq Semaines en Ballon · *See Five Weeks in a Balloon*

E

Extraordinary Voyages · 5, 11

F

Five Weeks in a Balloon · 3, 4, 29
From the Earth to the Moon · 5, 11, 16, 17, 23

Kathe Gust enjoys creating clothing for many historical periods, and for various sci-fi and fantasy genre. She has co-directed costume masquerades and served as a judge at the local, regional, and international levels. She served as International Costumers' Guild (ICG) Recording Secretary from 2012 to 2017.

As a member of the Silicon Web Costumers' Guild, she is the Secretary of the chapter, its Webmaster, and the Assistant Editor of the chapter's *The Virtual Costumer* quarterly online magazine (*https://siwcostumers.org/vc*),

She and husband Philip Gust received the ICG Lifetime Achievement Award in 2021. The award is the ICG's highest honor, recognizing a body of achievement in the costuming art and service to the costuming community. (*https://costume.org/wp/icg-lifetime-achievement-award/*)

She holds a Master of Science degree in Library Science and a Bachelor of Arts degree in Speech Communications.